REDISCOVERED ELLINGT

70 Great Ellington tunes arranged as

t Manager: Tony Esposito
Design: Odalis Soto

Contents

BLACK AND TAN FANTASY

By DUKE ELLINGTON
and BUBBER MILEY

fz
f
ff rit

MOOD INDIGO

By DUKE ELLINGTON, IRVING MILLS
and ALBANY BIGARD

3
rit.

NEW ORLEANS LOW DOWN

By DUKE ELLINGTON

mf
f
mf

3
f
mf

ff
f
marc.

WALL STREET WAIL

By DUKE ELLINGTON

mf

fz

ZONKY BLUES

By DUKE ELLINGTON

f

THE LAZY DUKE

By DUKE ELLINGTON

ff
fz

WASHINGTON WABBLE

By DUKE ELLINGTON

1
2
fz
mf
fz
ff

ff

FLAMING YOUTH

By DUKE ELLINGTON

l.h.
mp
cresc.
f l.h.
ff

3
l.h.
3
3
3
8
fz

HOP HEAD

By DUKE ELLINGTON

mf-f
3
1
2
ff

fz

SWEET MAMA

By DUKE ELLINGTON

3
3
3
3
3
3

MISTY MORNIN'

By ARTHUR WHETSEL
and DUKE ELLINGTON

1
2
f

BLUES I LOVE TO SING

By DUKE ELLINGTON
and BUBBER MILEY

1
2
fz
mf

ff
fz

GOIN' TO TOWN

By DUKE ELLINGTON
and BUBBER MILEY

Moderato

p
f
p
f

p
f
f

SWEET CHARIOT

By DUKE ELLINGTON
and IRVING MILLS

SLOPPY JOE

By DUKE ELLINGTON
and ALBANY BIGARD

Slow Drag Tempo

ff

AWFUL SAD

By DUKE ELLINGTON

BLACK CAT BLUES

By DUKE ELLINGTON

mf
f

mf
ff
3
3
fz

WHAT A LIFE!

By DUKE ELLINGTON

MEMPHIS WAIL

By DUKE ELLINGTON

B
1.
2.

BLUES OF THE VAGABOND

By DUKE ELLINGTON

3
f

f
3
3
3
fz

SOPHISTICATED LADY

By DUKE ELLINGTON

molto rit.

RUB-A-TUB-LUES

By DUKE ELLINGTON

ff
fz

BIRMINGHAM BREAK-DOWN

By DUKE ELLINGTON

f
fz

mf
ff
fz

MISSISSIPPI MOAN

By DUKE ELLINGTON

ff
fz

DICTY GLIDE

By DUKE ELLINGTON

ff
mf
f

3
3
3
3
fz

BLUE BUBBLES

By DUKE ELLINGTON

3
L. H.
p
cresc.
dim.
cresc.
dim.
cresc.
dim.
D. S. al Coda
CODA

JUBILEE STOMP

By DUKE ELLINGTON

to Coda

CODA

HARLEM FLAT BLUES

By DUKE ELLINGTON

f
ff l.h.
mf

DUCKY WUCKY

By DUKE ELLINGTON
and ALBANY BIGARD

Rythmé mais pas trop vite

ff

ff
ff

IMMIGRATION BLUES

By DUKE ELLINGTON

f
ff

tremolo
f-ff
fz

THE MOOCHE

By DUKE ELLINGTON
and IRVING MILLS

R.H.

3
1
R.H.
2
R.H.
R.H.

BLACK BEAUTY

By DUKE ELLINGTON

L. H.
R. H.
L. H.
L. H.

3
3
L.H.
8va

RENT PARTY BLUES

By DUKE ELLINGTON
and JOHNNY HODGES

ff

TAKE IT EASY

By DUKE ELLINGTON

L.H.

THE BREAKFAST DANCE

By DUKE ELLINGTON

mf
f

CINCINNATI DADDY

By DUKE ELLINGTON

f

MOVE OVER

By DUKE ELLINGTON

3
f
1.
2.
f

(♭)
(♮)
(♮)
3
3
f

DOIN' THE VOOM VOOM

By DUKE ELLINGTON
and BUBBER MILEY

f

mf

ROCKIN' IN RHYTHM

By DUKE ELLINGTON, IRVING MILLS
and HARRY CARNEY

mf
f

3
mf

rit.
pp

THE CREOLE LOVE CALL

By DUKE ELLINGTON

8
8
f
1.
2.
mf

3
3

EAST ST. LOUIS TOODLE-O

By DUKE ELLINGTON
and BUBBER MILEY

3
1
2
fz
f
1
2

3
3
fz

IT DON'T MEAN A THING

(If It Ain't Got That Swing)

By DUKE ELLINGTON

1
2
fz

BEST WISHES

By DUKE ELLINGTON

fz
V

SATURDAY NIGHT FUNCTION

By DUKE ELLINGTON
and ALBANY BIGARD

f
3
3
f
3
3
fz

THE BLUES WITH A FEELING

By DUKE ELLINGTON

Moderato

DROP ME OFF IN HARLEM

By DUKE ELLINGTON

1
2
fz

MOON OVER DIXIE

By DUKE ELLINGTON

fz

HIGH LIFE

By DUKE ELLINGTON

SYNCOPATED SHUFFLE

By DUKE ELLINGTON

THE MYSTERY SONG

By DUKE ELLINGTON
and IRVING MILLS

CHORUS
1.
2.

BATTLE OF SWING

By DUKE ELLINGTON

mf
mf

f
mp–mf
f
f

THE JEEP IS JUMPIN'

By DUKE ELLINGTON
and JOHNNY HODGES

mf
mf
mf

mf

BEAUTIFUL ROMANCE

By DUKE ELLINGTON
and COOTIE WILLIAMS

Rall.
Rit.

DRUMMER'S DELIGHT

By DUKE ELLINGTON
and ALBANY BIGARD

sfz
sfz

GAL-A-VANTIN'

By DUKE ELLINGTON
and COOTIE WILLIAMS

3
1
2

HODGE PODGE

By DUKE ELLINGTON
and JOHNNY HODGES

1
2

I'M IN ANOTHER WORLD

By DUKE ELLINGTON
and JOHNNY HODGES

mp-mf
1
2
rit

I'M RIDING ON THE MOON AND DANCING ON THE STARS

By DUKE ELLINGTON
and JOHNNY HODGES

1
2

JEEP'S BLUES

By DUKE ELLINGTON
and JOHNNY HODGES

1
2

PUSSY WILLOW

By DUKE ELLINGTON

1
2

PRELUDE TO A KISS

By DUKE ELLINGTON

mf
mf
mf
mf
1
2

PIGEONS AND PEPPERS

By DUKE ELLINGTON
and MERCER ELLINGTON

1
2
sfz

RIDING ON A BLUE NOTE

By DUKE ELLINGTON

mf
mf
mf
mf
1
2

SMORGASBORD AND SCHNAPPS

By DUKE ELLINGTON, REX STEWART
and BRICK FLEAGLE

ff
mf
ff
mf
1
2

STEPPIN' INTO SWING SOCIETY

By DUKE ELLINGTON

1
2

THE GAL FROM JOE'S

By DUKE ELLINGTON

1
2
sfz

WANDERLUST

By DUKE ELLINGTON
and JOHNNY HODGES

WAY LOW

By DUKE ELLINGTON

cresc
ff
f
p
pp calando
rall e dim
pp

YOU GAVE ME THE GATE

(And I'm Swingin')

By DUKE ELLINGTON

mp
1
2

WATERMELON MAN

By DUKE ELLINGTON

DUKE

We Love You Madly!